BALANCING ACCESS, COSTS, AND POLITICS

The American Context for Health System Reform

URBAN INSTITUTE REPORT 91–6

**John Holahan,
Marilyn Moon,
W. Pete Welch,
and Stephen Zuckerman**

THE URBAN INSTITUTE PRESS

Washington, D.C.

THE URBAN INSTITUTE PRESS

2100 M Street, N.W.
Washington, D.C. 20037

Library of Congress Cataloging in Publication Data

Balancing Access, Costs, and Politics: The American Context for Health System Reform / John Holahan. . .[et al.]

1. Medical policy—United States. 2. Medicare, Cost of—United States. 3. Medical care—United States. I. Holahan, John. II. Series.

RA395.A3B26	1991	91-16725
362.1'0973—dc20		CIP

(Urban Institute Reports; 91-6, ISSN 0897-7399)

ISBN 0-87766-518-4 (paper)
ISBN 0-87766-555-9 (cloth)

Printed in the United States of America.

Distributed by University Press of America

4720 Boston Way	3 Henrietta Street
Lanham, MD 20706	London WC2E 8LU
	ENGLAND

Urban Institute Reports are designed to provide rapid dissemination of research and policy findings. Each report contains timely information and is rigorously reviewed to uphold the highest standards of policy research and analysis.

The Urban Institute is a nonprofit policy research and educational organization established in Washington, D.C., in 1968. Its staff investigates the social and economic problems confronting the nation and government policies and programs designed to alleviate such problems. The Institute disseminates significant findings of its research through the publications program of its Press. The Institute has two goals for work in each of its research areas: to help shape thinking about societal problems and efforts to solve them, and to improve government decisions and performance by providing better information and analytic tools.

Through work that ranges from broad conceptual studies to administrative and technical assistance, Institute researchers contribute to the stock of knowledge available to public officials and private individuals and groups concerned with formulating and implementing more efficient and effective government policy.

Conclusions or opinions expressed in Institute publications are those of the authors and do not necessarily reflect the views of other staff members, officers or trustees of the Institute, advisory groups, or any organizations that provide financial support to the Institute.

ACKNOWLEDGMENTS

The authors are grateful to Judith Feder and Sheila Zedlewski for the detailed comments they provided on an earlier draft. In addition, we would like to acknowledge the patient assistance of Joan Sanders and Rebecca Hartman.

Support for this research was provided by Urban Institute General Funds. Opinions expressed in this document are those of the authors and do not necessarily represent the views of The Urban Institute or its sponsors.

CONTENTS

Tables

ABSTRACT

The U.S. health sector suffers from two major problems. Millions of Americans are without access to proper care because they lack adequate health insurance. And system costs are high and rapidly escalating. These are serious concerns and both are likely to get worse.

This report reviews the choices that must be made in developing any reform proposal and the criteria that should guide the choices. It lays out the advantages and disadvantages of alternative approaches, and evaluates the major reform proposals that have been put forward.

The authors then describe their own proposal, which is a combination of Medicare, employer mandates, and a state-based public program. Costs are controlled by legislative requirements regarding deductibles and coinsurance and by giving the states a substantial financial stake in ensuring that public program costs do not grow faster than general inflation. The approach allows considerable flexibility in designing competive and/or regulatory strategies for cost containment.

EXECUTIVE SUMMARY

Large numbers of uninsured Americans, high and rising health care costs, and administrative complexity are leading to many proposals aimed at reforming the United States' health care system. Some look to the Canadian system as a model for reform. Others view incremental policies such as expanding Medicaid as the most likely options. There is little consensus on what should be done.

The fundamental challenge facing any proposal is to significantly expand insurance coverage and control costs with policies that are politically acceptable. Proposals that threaten well-established interest groups will face opposition. The issue of how much of the health care system should be in the public sector is also a matter that must be adequately addressed. Although a highly centralized system with stringent government controls could tackle health system problems directly, as under the Canadian system, U.S. reliance on a market system for allocating most goods and services represents a strongly held philosophy favoring diversity and indirect incentives and controls.

The most visible U.S. policy proposal—presented by The Pepper Commission last year—would require firms with more than 100 employees to provide health insurance or pay a tax to cover the costs of enrolling their employees in a public plan—a "pay or play" approach. In addition, the Pepper Commission would eliminate experience rating in private health insurance and establish nationally uniform eligibility and payment policies for Medicaid.

This study assesses the advantages and disadvantages of various approaches to reform. It concludes that although the Canadian approach is attractive in that it provides universal coverage and controls costs better than the U.S. system, it is not a serious option for the United States. Unwillingness to incur the large public sector costs, eliminate the private health insurance industry, and establish uniform cost containment policies, are major reasons why the United States will not adopt a Canadian-style system. The Pepper Commission proposal is more feasible politically, but would initially leave some Americans without health insurance and provide only weak cost containment incentives.

Building on the strengths of both the Canadian system and the Pepper Commission proposal, this report developes a plan that encompasses a uniquely American approach to health system reform. The proposal would keep Medicare as is. It would implement the "pay or play" feature of the Pepper commission but it would cover virtually all small businesses and provide greater subsidies for the near poor. A state-administered public plan, which would replace Medicaid, would cover the poor, families, and individuals whose employers chose to pay the tax, and all others who choose to privately "buy-in" to the public plan. The tax rate for employers not providing private insurance would be set so that approximately one-third of the non-elderly population was in the public plan. The federal government would share in the costs of the public plan, but the federal contribution would be limited to increases no faster than the growth in the Gross National Product. States would be responsible for costs in excess of the federal contribution, providing a strong incentive for them to control costs. Choosing the appropriate cost containment policy would be left to the states to ensure flexibility and to allow the testing of different mechanisms.

Administration of the private programs would remain with employers and/or insurance companies, while states would be responsible for administering the public program. A standard minimum package of benefits would be required for employer-based and public programs. The test of political feasibility would be met by retaining a major role for insurance companies and for employer-based coverage, thus reducing the tax increase needed to ensure universal coverage.

This proposal is not without its problems, which include adverse effects on the profitability of small businesses and on the employment prospects of low-wage workers; unwillingness or lack of ability of some states to carry out a public program; and a visible increase in taxes at the federal and state levels. We believe, however, that such costs are less than those incurred by other proposals, and that they are a modest price to pay for resolving the problem of the uninsured and for gaining control over skyrocketing health care costs.

Chapter

1

PROBLEMS WITH THE U.S. HEALTH SYSTEM

The U.S. health care system does an excellent job of treating patients: Symptoms are reviewed, tests conducted, diagnoses made, and a course of treatment planned. However, when the "patient" is the health care system itself, the process seems to break down. Despite consensus on the diagnoses—acutely high and rising costs and chronic access problems—the condition is not yet perceived as serious enough to force agreement on a treatment plan. While options abound, none has emerged as the most clearly defensible and politically acceptable. This paper explores the strengths and weaknesses of alternative approaches and presents a plan that solves the access problems of the current system, while at the same time allowing for the experimentation required to find effective solutions for our health care cost problems.[1]

This chapter describes the two fundamental problems with the current system—gaps in coverage and escalating costs. The second chapter reviews the choices that must be made in developing any reform proposal and how those choices are now being made. The third chapter reviews alternative approaches to resolving access and cost problems and lays out the advantages and disadvantages of the major reform proposals that have been put forward. All these proposals either fail to provide universal coverage or to provide strong cost containment incentives. The final chapter describes a proposal that accomplishes both through a combination of Medicare, employer mandates, and a state-based public system.

THE UNINSURED

At least 31 million Americans lacked even the most basic health insurance in 1987 (Monhiet and Short 1989; Moyer 1989; Swartz 1989; Zedlewski 1991). An even larger number are without health insurance for some period during the year (Nelson and Short 1990). Although the uninsured include the poor and unemployed as well as the homeless and drug abusers, two-thirds of the uninsured live in households where the head is a full-time worker (Holahan and Zedlewski 1991). These households include large numbers of dependents not covered by employee plans, as well as employees of both large and small firms, and self-employed workers. In addition to those Americans with no health insurance, millions more have insurance coverage that could be inadequate in the case of serious illness (Farley 1985).

Health care coverage in the United States comes from two major sources—employers and public programs.

Employer-based insurance is being eroded by the rising costs of care. The percentage of premiums paid by employers has gradually fallen, while cost-sharing requirements have grown (DiCarlo and Gabel 1988). Moreover, the cost of insuring workers, particularly low-wage workers, has led some employers to raise the employee contributions to levels that more and more workers are increasingly unwilling or unable to pay (U.S. Department of Labor, Bureau of Labor Statistics 1990). In addition, some persons with major health problems are unable to purchase insurance at any cost.

Public programs in the United States cover some groups but not others. The main public health coverage programs are Medicare and Medicaid. The federal Medicare program covers almost all persons over 65 years of age and about 3 million disabled persons. State Medicaid programs cover slightly over half the nonelderly poor (Holahan and Zedlewski 1991). But because Medicaid has historically been tied to public assistance, low-income mothers and young children are more likely to be covered than are fathers, older children, or single adults. The distribution of Medicaid coverage is also geographically uneven. States that have historically been generous in providing Medicaid coverage have lower numbers of uninsured and vice versa (Holahan and Zedlewski 1991).

Lack of health insurance coverage results in poor access and low levels of utilization (Robert Wood Johnson Foundation 1987). This has led to recent efforts to expand Medicaid coverage for pregnant women and children. Lack of coverage also causes major problems for hospitals, because of the inability of some patients to pay for care they have received. If these unpaid bills result in higher hospital charges, the result will be increases in private health insurance premiums, both employer-based and individual coverage. Hospitals unable to finance this care must reduce services or face financial losses and perhaps closure. In such cases, all persons in the area served by such a hospital may ultimately be affected.

ESCALATING COSTS

Health care expenditures in the United States are substantially higher than in any other nation. As shown in table 1.1, the U.S. spent over $2,000 per person in 1987. In contrast, Canada spent $1,515, and other nations spent significantly less. Table 1.1 also shows that spending for health care in the United States in the 1980s has grown at annual rates in excess of 10 percent. Nearly half of this growth is due to the rate of increase in general inflation. The remainder, almost 5 percent per year, is due to an increase in real spending per capita. In real terms, our health care expenditure growth is also outpacing that of most other industrialized countries. It is doubly ironic that we spend substantially more per capita at the same time that we exclude a significant proportion of citizens from the mainstream of our health care system.

As table 1.2 shows, spending relative to Gross Domestic Product (GDP) is at least 2 percentage points higher in the United States than in any other industrialized nation. Note in particular Canada. In 1970, when Canada adopted universal health insurance, both Canada and the United States spent slightly more than 7 percent of GDP on health. By 1987, the proportion had grown to 8.8 percent of GDP in Canada compared with 11.2 percent in the United States.

Thus, over the last two decades Canada has been much more successful than the United States in keeping the growth in its health care costs in line with its economic growth. In comparing health care expenditures across nations, two measures are used: the growth in the percentage of the GDP spent on health care and the growth

Table 1.1 GROWTH IN HEALTH EXPENDITURES IN
SELECTED INDUSTRIALIZED COUNTRIES:
1980-1987

Country	1987	1980-1987	
	Annual Expenditures per Capita in U.S. Dollars	Annual Change in Actual Health Expenditures	Annual Change in Health Expenditures, Adjusted for Inflation and Population Growth
U.S.	$2,051	10.5%	4.8%
Canada	1,515	11.3	4.7
France	1,090	11.4	2.9
W. Germany	1,073	4.7	1.7
Netherlands	1,038	4.1	1.2
Japan	917	6.1	3.9
UK	746	9.3	2.8

Source: George J. Schieber and Jean-Pierre Poulier. 1989. "Overview of International Comparisons of Health Care Expenditures." *Health Care Financing Review* 11, no. 1 (Fall); Jean-Pierre Poulier. 1989. "Health Care Expenditures and Other Data." *Health Care Financing Review* 11, no. 1 (Fall).

in health care expenditures per capita. The Health Insurance Association of America (HIAA) has recently argued that while Canada has performed better than the U.S. in terms of the former, this is completely due to differences in GDP growth, and that increases in real health expen-

Table 1.2   EXPENDITURES AS A PERCENTAGE OF
GROSS DOMESTIC PRODUCT IN SELECTED
INDUSTRIALIZED COUNTRIES: 1970-1987

Country	1970	1980	1987
US	7.4	9.2	11.2
Canada	7.2	7.4	8.8
France	5.8	7.6	8.5
W. Germany	5.5	7.9	8.1
Netherlands	6.0	8.2	8.5
Japan	4.4	6.4	6.8
UK	4.5	5.8	6.1

Source: George J. Schieber and Jean-Pierre Poulier. 1989. "Overview of International Comparisons of Health Care Expenditures." *Health Care Financing Review* 11, no. 1 (Fall); Jean-Pierre Poulier. 1989. "Health Care Expenditures and Other Data." *Health Care Financing Review* 11, no. 1 (Fall).

ditures per capita have been virtually identical. HIAA argues that the latter is the appropriate comparison; we believe this argument is incorrect. Health care spending and GDP growth are not independent. As GDP grows, the incomes paid to all factors of production increase. Unless real output in a sector were falling, spending can be expected to increase at about the same rate as GDP. This means that the higher rate of growth in Canadian GDP should have resulted in higher rates of growth in health care spending than in the United States, even if both countries were equally successful (or unsuccessful) in controlling costs. The fact that Canadians contained health spending to the growth in their economy suggests that Canada has indeed been successful in controlling its costs. In contrast, health care in the U.S. has been absorbing an increasing share of a more slowly growing GDP.

Of all the reasons given for the high costs of the U.S. health care system, three stand out. One is the high administrative costs of a mixed private/public system (Evans et al. 1989; Himmelstein and Woolhandler 1986). These include the costs of selling insurance policies, the costs of determining eligibility for benefits and filing claims with disparate insurers, and the high administrative costs imposed on beneficiaries. The second reason is widespread diffusion of health care technology in the United States (Evans 1986). Reliance on this technology often constitutes an add-on to physician visits and treatment that increases rather than saves on cost. Finally, because of both high utilization and high service prices, the incomes of health care providers, particularly physicians, are extremely high relative to those in other nations (Fuchs and Hahn 1990).

The problems of cost and lack of insurance coverage are closely related. As noted, higher costs have reduced the numbers of employers offering health coverage to their workers. And some employers who continue to provide coverage have shifted more of the cost to their employees in the form of higher premiums, fewer benefits, and higher deductibles and coinsurance (GAO 1990; Dicarlo and Gabel 1989). Public sector costs have also increased rapidly, putting pressure on federal and state governments to control costs by reducing access and/or services covered. The rate of growth remains high despite the many cost-containment measures that have been tried.

HOW HAVE THESE PROBLEMS DEVELOPED?

The systemic and persistent problems of maintaining access and controlling costs have evolved as our health care system has evolved—piecemeal. Employer-based health insurance began in the 1930s. During World War II, employer-based health insurance expanded rapidly because adding it as a fringe benefit allowed employers to increase workers' compensation without violating strict wartime wage and price controls. As a fringe benefit, these premiums were deductible as a business expense and not taxable as income. After the war, the growth in employer-based insurance continued as labor unions bargained collectively for health benefits (Starr 1982).

An essential gap in this system was the lack of provision for individuals without employment to acquire adequate and affordable health care protection. In addition, people were routinely forced to change their source of health insurance when they changed jobs. In 1965 the public sector provided a partial solution to the first problem through the introduction of Medicare and Medicaid. Medicare provided nationally uniform comprehensive coverage for all elderly Americans. Medicaid was a federal and state financed, state-administered program that offered varying coverage to a narrowly defined segment of the poor. Individuals without employer-based group insurance who did not qualify for Medicare or Medicaid had the choice of attempting to purchase insurance on their own or remaining uninsured. Despite the growth of public programs, this choice still faces many Americans today.

In the 1970s and 1980s, even though a substantial number of Americans remained uninsured, state and federal policymakers turned their attention away from access to the growing problem of health care costs. Costs grew rapidly because most people did not pay the full costs of the services they received, and had little incentive to seek out the lowest-priced providers. Efforts to promote efficiency in this type of market drew on two basic remedies—regulation of provider behavior, or stimulation of a competitive environment by giving consumers a greater stake in the costs of care.

Initially, regulation was administered by the states, whose efforts to control costs focused on hospitals as the largest health care providers. With federal support, policies were established that directly controlled the volume and distribution of capital investment through certificate-of-need laws and requirements for prior approval of large outlays. In addition, states developed a variety of systems to establish limits on hospital spending. By the early 1980s, some of these policy approaches were being adopted by the federal government, notably in Medicare's prospective payment system (PPS) for hospitals. PPS pays a fixed amount for a particular diagnosis—a major departure from simply paying whatever costs were incurred for each patient. However, other parts of the health care sector that account for substantial amounts of spending, such as physicians, have gone virtually unregulated.

Efforts to stimulate competition have been pursued on several fronts. To try to make individuals more cost-conscious, for example, a growing number of employers and insurers have increased the amount of consumer cost sharing. Employers have also begun requiring more employees to pay at least part of their premiums. Another component of policies to increase competition has involved the nurturing of low-cost providers. To this end the federal government enacted the Health Maintenance Organization (HMO) Act of 1973 as a means of giving a potentially efficient alternative health care provider a chance to gain acceptance. Though HMO market shares have increased, they remain well below the hopes of their early supporters. More recently, preferred provider organizations (PPOs), which reward consumers for selecting low-cost providers, have begun to proliferate (Board of Trustees of Federal Hospital Insurance Trust Fund 1990). However, as with regulation, competitive solutions are pursued differently by different payers. Generally, only large payers have been able to force providers to compete effectively.

Thus, the problems with U.S. health care are rooted in the piecemeal evolution of the system. The gaps in coverage result from the fundamental nature of employer-based insurance and the limited targeted approach of existing public programs. Efforts to contain costs have been varied and widespread, but not widely successful. Much of the blame appears to rest with the fragmented, multiple-payer structure of the system.

WHY THE CRISIS WILL GET WORSE

The problems discussed here are serious. However, they have not yet led to widespread demands by the public for reform of the health care financing system. The divided response to the recently released Pepper Commission proposals is the latest example of this. Not only is there disagreement about how to respond to existing problems, but the situation is not yet perceived as sufficiently serious to bring the relevant actors together to compromise on basic reform.

This perception is likely to be short-lived. Current cost and access problems will almost certainly get worse and harder to fix. The premiums currently paid by those with private insurance are likely to increase. These premiums are rising both for traditional reasons (e.g., increasing utilization at least partially related to the introduction of new technologies) and because of the growing volume of uncompensated care being demanded from the system. The premium burden will be borne increasingly by patients with limited market power, disproportionately affecting individuals who work in small businesses or those who have individually purchased non-group insurance. In an effort to escape rising premiums, these individuals may choose less coverage, both in terms of benefits and cost sharing, leaving them increasingly exposed to financial catastrophe should illness strike.

As costs rise, high-risk patients will find it more and more difficult to obtain insurance under any circumstances. Even firms with a generally healthy population but some high-risk patients will face particularly sharp increases in premiums and may be unable to obtain insurance at all. If firms that continue to offer job-related coverage shift the premium burden onto their employees via lower real wages, they will face increasing labor disputes about health insurance coverage.

The second problem is that the number of uninsured is likely to grow. As the cost of private health insurance increases, more and more employers may stop offering insurance coverage, limit the kinds of insurance offered, and/or increase employee contributions to premiums—all actions that reflect a desire to reduce the employer's financial stake and shift the burden to the employee. More and more employees will not be able to afford insurance coverage in these circumstances. Dependent coverage, in particular, will continue to shrink.

The third factor aggravating the crisis is that Medicare and Medicaid will face the same spiraling health care costs as the private sector. Expenditure growth in Medicare is projected to substantially exceed revenue growth in the coming decade, creating major fiscal problems. An aging population, higher hospital input costs, rising physician fees, and the introduction of new technologies will all contribute to this trend. Medicare's prospective payment system (PPS) for hospitals and controls on growth in physician fees have had some effect. But few analysts believe that further cuts in Medicare payment rates will be simple to achieve. A more likely outcome is continuing increases in Medicare costs—requiring higher premiums, higher payroll taxes, and/or larger contributions from general revenue. None of these results will be politically popular. Medicaid is in a similar situation. States have been fairly successful in keeping Medicaid cost growth close to the rate of inflation, but this will become increasingly difficult if even modest levels of access are to be maintained.

An economic slowdown is likely to exacerbate all of these problems. A recession may result in more uninsured as employers lay off workers or further cut back on their insurance contribution. It will also further limit states' willingness to expand Medicaid to cover more of the uninsured poor, as well as the chronically ill and disabled. The recent demands from state governors that

Congress cease expanding Medicaid mandates is an indication of state resistance to further Medicaid expansions.

The combination of cost and access pressures will also exact a toll on providers of health care, especially hospitals. Medicare PPS has progressively tightened payment rates to hospitals (ProPAC 1990). Private sector success in negotiating rates with hospitals will limit the ability of hospitals to impose higher charges on private patients. Hospitals will still retain this ability to some degree, but fewer and fewer privately insured individuals will be able to pay these charges. At the same time, hospital input costs will increase due to general wage inflation and the introduction of new technologies. The growing number of high-cost uninsured persons—such as AIDS patients, the homeless, and drug abusers—will constitute a rising burden for many hospitals. The only recourse for these hospitals will be to cut back on services. This could have the effect of eliminating trauma units and emergency rooms as hospitals attempt to avoid hard-to-care-for, nonpaying patients. Finally, the hospitals under the worst financial pressures will eventually close. In cases where hospitals are the primary or sole source of care and a principal employer, their closing will have major implications for their communities, spreading the problems beyond the uninsured and the employers who pay the premiums.

If these problems do in fact worsen, more serious debate will result and an increasing willingness to compromise could emerge. Yet, how to reform the system to solve the problems of cost and access is no simple question. The wide variety of proposals and the lack to date of any consensus partially reflects the fact that the financial and ideological stakes involved are quite large. There are advantages and disadvantages to all the proposals, and tradeoffs are inevitable. In an effort to assess how these tradeoffs might best be made, the next chapter lays out the major dimensions that must be considered in designing a reform proposal, and describes how the current U.S. system fares along each dimension.

Note, chapter 1

1. Although the absence of an effective insurance system for long-term care is also thought to be a major problem with the U.S. health system, this issue is beyond the scope of this report.

2

THE DIMENSIONS OF HEALTH CARE SYSTEM REFORM

In this chapter, we review six questions regarding health care system reform that any serious proposal must address. These are:

- Who is covered? To what extent will access be expanded?

- How are costs controlled?

- Who pays? How is the system financed?

- What benefits are covered?

- Who administers and ultimately oversees the day-to-day management of the system? and

- Is the proposal politically feasible?

Given the problems outlined in the previous chapter, the first two questions clearly touch on the central issues. However, the remaining questions embody specific issues that will determine whether any individual proposal will ever be adopted. The remainder of this chapter reviews the possible answers to these questions.

WHO IS COVERED?

One of the most basic choices for health system reform is which groups to cover. A system may be universal, ensuring that all Americans are covered, or it may allow most people to arrange for their own insurance while targeting certain subgroups of the population, such as the poor or children, for guaranteed coverage.

Under the current system three groups of Americans are covered: individuals who purchase private insurance or whose employers offer subsidized insurance, the very poor who meet certain eligibility criteria for Medicaid coverage, and persons over 65 and some of the disabled, both of whom are covered by Medicare. The groups that fall through the cracks are the poor or near poor who do not meet the eligibility criteria for Medicaid, working families with modest incomes for whom employer-provided coverage is either unavailable or unaffordable, and the uninsured with higher incomes. This last group is generally of less concern to policymakers.

A universal approach is often thought to imply a single system of uniform coverage. For example, a Canadian-type system, where the government acts as the insurer, achieves universal coverage with essentially a single system in each province. But universal coverage can also be achieved by a combination of public and private approaches. For instance, one could reach universal coverage through a combination of employer mandates and an expanded public sector plan available for those with low incomes.

Targeted approaches, on the other hand, are intended to fill in gaps that exist in the current system. Targeted approaches in the U.S. context are generally offered as a means for limiting interference in the provision of health insurance that now occurs through employment. Proponents of targeting typically focus only on part of the uninsured, usually those who cannot afford to purchase private health insurance and/or those classified as "uninsurable" because of existing health problems.

If affordability of insurance is the only concern of policymakers, providing insurance coverage through a public plan or subsidizing enrollment in a private one can solve the problem. Since the current Medicaid program falls far short of covering all the poor, however, many more individuals would need to be supported through a public subsidy. Private sector approaches would require public subsidies because some fundamental redistribution of income is required.

Sometimes the targeted group is individuals who find themselves excluded from group plans and unable to purchase individual coverage because they are identified as high medical risks. One frequently proposed solution for high-risk groups is the creation of risk pools, usually at the state level, to make subsidized insurance available for these individuals—either by requiring contributions from insurance companies, in which case costs would be transferred to purchasers of private insurance, or by increasing the burden on taxpayers.

Targeted approaches may go beyond filling in gaps in coverage. Entire classes of individuals could be covered if society decides this is appropriate. Such targeting extends beyond narrow welfare-type programs and defines as eligible all individuals who meet the standards. The elderly have traditionally constituted such a group. Medicare remains a program the public views with great favor. It has been suggested that Medicare could be expanded to include all children and pregnant women. Better coverage for children, before and after birth, could pay off later by improving the overall, long-term health of these individuals. These types of targeted groups are easier to define and require less administrative oversight of eligibility than groups targeted by means-tested (welfare) programs. Some advocates of broader coverage also view this type of targeted approach as a way to test the feasibility of broader national insurance plans.

The limits placed on how far to go with any of the targeted approaches to expansion nearly always turn on the costs to the public sector. Furthermore, targeted proposals, as noted, rarely extend beyond coverage of the very poor or very sick.

HOW ARE COSTS CONTROLLED?

Cost containment is becoming a major consideration in health system design, although the best means to achieve it remain subject to considerable disagreement. In the United States, no concerted effort to control all health care costs exists. Individual insurers or employers often seek to find ways to hold down their own costs, but this has often meant merely shifting the burden to others. For example, an employer or insurer may raise cost-sharing and premium contributions to save its own resources, while shifting the burden onto its employees. Although higher patient cost sharing may reduce use, it largely reduces costs to the employer by shifting the responsibility onto the employees.

Some parts of the U.S. health care system have benefited from the introduction of alternatives to traditional fee-for-service providers as a means of controlling costs. However, at present, these alternatives—Preferred Provider Organizations (PPOs), Individual Practice Associations (IPAs), and Health Maintenance Organizations (HMOs)—have a limited market share.[1] There have been efforts to control hospital costs through regulation. Some states, for example, have been operating rate-setting systems for hospitals and have had success in controlling hospital costs (Eby and Cohodes 1985). At the national level, as noted, the Medicare program introduced its prospective payment system (PPS) for hospitals in the early 1980s and has achieved some success in changing the behavior of the nation's hospitals.

A fundamental decision about the future direction of cost containment is whether to focus on the patient or the provider as the source of cost control. Requiring further patient cost sharing through deductibles or copayments is often advocated by those who believe that patients must bear at least part of the responsibility, and that the volume of services delivered under the U.S. health care system is excessive because Americans do not have to pay enough of the cost at the point of service.

Research indicates that cost sharing does affect utilization. For example, The RAND Corporation's health insurance experiment demonstrated that copayment by patients has a relatively small but significant effect on health care utilization. More importantly, the RAND experiment also found that the impact of copayments was no greater for inappropriate care than for appropriate care, calling into question the use of increased cost sharing as a rationing mechanism (Lohr et al. 1986). In fact, most other industrialized countries do not rely heavily on cost sharing as a mechanism for cost containment, and (as was shown in tables 1.1 and 1.2) have had uniformly better experience than the United States in controlling costs.

The options for controlling costs through providers fall into two types: regulation, and using the market to foster competition to reduce costs. The most direct approach to controlling costs through the provider side of the market involves regulatory activities. One regulatory approach is to subject all providers to the same rate-setting system. This approach uses the monopsony power of a large buyer, presumably but not necessarily the government, to control prices paid to hospitals and physicians, and to put volume limits on services. This approach could also be used to control the rate of diffusion of technological innovations. Such an arrangement is used in Canada, in which the government is a single payer. But rate-setting is also possible in a health care system with multiple insurers, as in many European countries. Separate insurers could all be required to pay rates established by the government as "rate setter," or could contribute to a fund through which a single payer would make all payments to providers.

The main strength of this approach is that it introduces a de facto monopsonist—the rate setter—to counterbalance the behavioral tendencies of health care providers, who are often viewed as having some monopoly power over health care decisions. But regulation can also have

This has not been the case in other places.

drawbacks. If the regulator is highly effective at controlling the expansion of health care spending, new and potentially beneficial technologies may get introduced more slowly. Viewed in a different, positive light, restricting technology may in fact be one successful regulatory approach. On the other hand, a regulatory system may be rendered ineffective if providers are able to influence key decisions by "capturing" the regulators.

More indirect approaches of encouraging competition as a way to lower prices reflect Americans' preference for choice and the marketplace over government intervention. Theoretically, competitors will offer lower prices and higher quality to attract customers.

One approach to cost control that works through the market is called "managed competition." Managed competition seeks to control costs through competition among multiple, managed care arrangements such as HMOs, IPAs, and PPOs, with consumers able to choose those programs that offer the most for their money. The assumption is that such competition lowers costs to the point where traditional indemnity arrangements are no longer competitive. Ideally, physicians join at least one managed care organization in order to assure access to a sufficient number of patients. Managed care organizations would fail if they did not have sufficient market power to gain access to enough physicians or to gain sufficient discounts with hospitals. The competition among the remaining successful managed care organizations would give the system control over provider payment rates and volume. Universal access to health care could be assured if national policy required everyone to enroll in a managed care organization, with subsidies if necessary.

The negative side of competition arises when providers seek ways to screen out the bad risks, thereby voiding the benefits of price competition. Such providers may get away with lower costs, but only by leaving the care of costly patients to others. To avoid this and other problems with competition, such as elimination of services that are cost effective to society but are infrequently required, most advocates of this approach call for oversight of these market activities.

WHO PAYS?

Any system allocates the responsibility for health coverage among three groups in society: employers—through contributions on behalf of their employees; taxpayers—through a government-funded public program; and individuals—through premium contributions or cost sharing. In our highly fragmented health care system all three groups pay for health care under myriad disguises. Employers undertake a considerable share of the costs, although the amount paid for particular workers depends on both the generosity of the firm and factors that influence the cost of insurance, such as firm size and region. Employees also pay a considerable share of the costs themselves through premium contributions and out-of-pocket costs for use of uncovered services. (This initial responsibility does not necessarily stay with these same groups. For example, employers are likely to shift the costs of health insurance back on to employees in the form of lower wages or slower wage growth over time.)

Taxpayers pay a substantial share of U.S. health care costs. Tax revenues directly support Medicare and Medicaid, the chief health programs for the aged, disabled, and poor. In addition, the government indirectly helps finance private employer-based health insurance coverage through tax benefits offered to employers and employees. In particular, by allowing employer-paid health premiums to be offered tax free, employees have strong incentives to seek health benefits in lieu of higher pay. Taxpayers also directly pay some of the costs of care for low-income individuals receiving care in public hospitals and clinics. Finally, some care is paid very indirectly by users of the system who must pay higher charges to help hospitals afford charity care.

Whatever choices are made under system reform, individuals ultimately bear the costs. But the choice will determine how the overall burden is distributed. Publicly financed systems have the advantage of allowing decisions about who will pay because of the ability to alter the progressiveness of the tax system. It is easier to ensure that people with like abilities to pay are asked to make like contributions through a tax structure than through other alternatives.

Relying on employers to pay much of the costs of care has the advantage of being "off the books" politically speaking. In an era of fiscal austerity and reluctance to raise taxes, having employers rather than taxpayers pay is an important plus. Moreover, since employers are already a major source of health care financing in the United States, maintaining the status quo is easier than shifting all financing to a new system.

Cost sharing, or direct payments for part or all of the costs of care, can be used as a method of deciding who pays as well as a way to control costs. The higher the cost sharing, the greater the burden on the patient and his/her family and the less burden on the general taxpayer and employer. This, of course, means that cost sharing imposes its burden on the sick, in contrast to employee contributions or tax burdens, which are paid equally by the sick and the well. Most proposals that cover more of the low-income uninsured or those in poor health also call for limits on patient cost sharing with the balance coming from taxpayer subsidies.

WHAT ARE THE BENEFITS?

There is little disagreement that certain benefits such as hospital inpatient and outpatient care and a considerable range of physician services should be covered in any insurance arrangement. But beyond the basics there is serious disagreement over what types of care or treatment should be covered. On the one hand, some sorts of treatment are often thought to be overused when fully covered, making very generous benefit packages expensive. On the other hand, denying coverage for items that are an essential part of a patient's treatment may actually result in higher treatment costs over time. Moreover, benefits used intensively by a small number of patients might need to be covered to avoid problems of adverse selection—avoidance by insurers of high risk patients. Unless such benefits are in the basic plan, no private insurers would be likely to offer such coverage.

Coverage varies enormously in the United States depending on the generosity of the payer. Medicare, as well as traditional private health insurance, typically covers a relatively standard package of services. There is much greater variety among plans in coverage of mental health care, dental services, chiropractors, podiatrists, and optometrists. Many states also mandate the inclusion of particular types of health care coverage in standard insurance packages. In response to these mandates, many employers "self-insure" so that they can put together their own benefit package and avoid premium taxes and the constraints they would face if they contracted for a standard insurance package. State Medicaid benefits also vary substantially across the country, both because states offer different options and because the generosity of the reimbursement structure influences the number of providers willing to participate in the Medicaid program.

Prescription drugs and mental health services are particularly contentious parts of the debate on coverage reform in the United States. These are important services, but ones that can add substantially to costs. The dilemma with prescription drugs is that, on the one hand, they are extremely expensive, and the administrative costs of processing claims are also extremely high. On the other hand, certain medications are essential for ensuring the effectiveness of physician and other services. If appropriate drugs are not used, the overall costs of care may rise. It is inconsistent, for example, to cover physician visits and then not cover the drugs prescribed.

Mental health care poses a similar dilemma. These services are critical for a small number of beneficiaries. However, lengthy periods of treatment for mental health problems can be extremely expensive. Broad coverage of mental health benefits also increases the risk of adverse selection in private insurance arrangements.

One alternative approach to coverage restrictions is to limit coverage of specific procedures. The Oregon state legislature, for example, is attempting to implement this approach to limit services covered under Medicaid (Morrell 1990). A committee of physicians and citizens now has the power to rank health care services according to the perceived effectiveness of the service relative to its cost. Given a budget constraint, for instance, the amount the citizenry are willing to spend, the legislature can choose to cover only those services deemed to be most effective. More recently, the approach has initially identified some targets for elimination, such as organ transplants, cosmetic surgery, and restorative dentistry. However, these easy targets do not involve a substantial proportion of the Medicaid budget. Most health care resources go for basic office and hospital visits, routine as well as specialized tests, major and minor surgery, and high technology diagnostic services (Berenson and Holahan 1990). The decisions required to rank these procedures by effectiveness and cost are likely to be difficult to make.

A second alternative approach to the coverage issue, related to the cost containment and payment issues mentioned above, is to vary how much patients should be asked to contribute to the cost of the covered service. For example, cost sharing could be higher for services that are not traditionally included in a basic package or whose clinical effectiveness is open to question. But low-income patients may be unable or unwilling to seek care if the cost sharing component is major.

A third way of altering coverage is to limit the degree of patient choice over the providers from whom they can receive care. If patients are required by their public or private insurance to join a managed care plan, such as an HMO or PPO, their choice of physicians and hospitals will be restricted. Such organizations can effectively alter the mix of services that patients receive.

WHO ADMINISTERS?

Closely related to the issue of who pays is who controls and oversees the health care system. Under the current system, whoever pays for the care typically has administrative responsibility, but there is little coordination of payment or use of services beyond the immediate payer. The result is a system with few abilities to control costs or to redirect resources to where they are most needed. The exception to this occurs in a few states that take a more active role in overseeing and regulating health care for everyone.

Generally, we assume those who are financially responsible are also the managers of any program, but this does not necessarily need be the case. For example, funding could be provided publicly by giving tax deductions to employers or vouchers to individuals to support insurance costs. Taxpayers would be footing the bill, but employers or individuals would still be responsible for managing the insurance by determining coverage and negotiating with insurance companies for the best policies.

Another example of separating funding and administration would occur in a system where the federal government, through taxes, would generate most of the revenues to support a public program but would leave administration to the states. Such a system could correct for the substantial differences in the abilities of states to subsidize the health needs of the poor and uninsured, while preserving a system that reflects the political realities across states. It could also exploit a good feature of our current system—the ability of the states to experiment with different approaches to the problem of achieving expanded access within the constraints of controlling costs. The danger of less than direct linkage between financing and oversight, however, is a system with few incentives for cost control.

WHAT IS POLITICALLY FEASIBLE?

It is unrealistic to offer health care reforms that have no political support or raise such formidable political obstacles that they could not be enacted into law in the foreseeable future. Thus, anyone who believes the need for health care system reform is urgent has the responsibility to choose a health reform package that meets the test of political feasibility.

At least two elements determine feasibility. First, any reform that threatens well-established interest groups such as the provider community and insurance companies will face great opposition. It should be noted in this connection that some providers have shown more willingness to accept controls than others. For example, hospitals in the United States are already accustomed to substantial intervention and oversight. In contrast, the prescription drug industry has sent strong signals that it would rather not be covered under any government program than face close scrutiny. And insurance companies, as well as many Americans with private insurance, are very sensitive to whether a meaningful role would be left for the private sector under a reformed health care system.

Second, the issue of how much of any health care system ought to be in the public sector is very troublesome. The American public is likely to resist substantially higher taxes to cover a large program. There is also likely to be ideological resistance to a large public system even if such a system might operate more efficiently than the current one. On the one hand, a highly centralized health care system, with stringent government controls, could tackle health system problems directly. On the other hand, U.S. reliance on a market system for allocating most goods and services represents a strongly held philosophy favoring diversity and indirect incentives and controls.

Note, chapter 2

1. HMOs are large prepaid group practice organizations that both assume risk and provide services with a closed panel of physicians and hospitals. IPAs are HMOs that provide care through looser groupings of independent physicians who agree to reduce fees and controls over utilization. PPOs are even looser organizations, which function by signing agreements with a number of physicians in a geographic area, offering them access to the PPO's patient membership in return for negotiated fees and utilization controls. Beneficiaries can choose to use physicians in the PPO network or, by accepting greater cost sharing, can use physicians and hospitals out of the network.

3

CURRENT PROPOSALS FOR HEALTH CARE REFORM

S ince the U.S. health care system is widely recognized to have serious problems, reform proposals abound—even though there is no consensus on the best approach. The policy choices range from one extreme of making minimal changes (essentially what has happened so far), to the other extreme of implementing national health insurance on the Canadian model, where there is a single public payer but providers remain private and independent. Public hospitals and clinics already exist and might be expanded as well, but the debate over national health insurance in the United States nearly always excludes the option of full nationalization or "socialization" of medical care, under which the providers themselves would be public entities.

In this chapter we look at the major proposals currently being debated. We start with the simplest proposals and move to the most complex. We ignore the minimalist approach of simple regulatory reform to eliminate arbitrary discrimination in the insurance market. Such an approach would do little to control costs or to increase access for the poor or medically indigent.

In the final chapter of this report we propose an alternative that combines some key features of the Canadian system with selected components of the other approaches currently being discussed in the U.S.

EXPANDING MEDICAID

Expansion of the Medicaid program, which is a targeted approach to expanding access, was proposed by President Bush in the 1988 presidential election, as well as in his first State of the Union Address.

Congress has already expanded Medicaid in recent years to cover pregnant women and children, a move that has eliminated the link between Medicaid and welfare for these groups and has permitted states to raise these groups' income eligibility levels. Further Medicaid expansions could include increased coverage of these population groups and coverage of the remainder of the poor and near-poor. One option is to cover the poor up to 100 percent of poverty and permit the non-poor to buy into Medicaid based on a sliding-scale premium related to income.

The advantages of expanding Medicaid are numerous. Additional government spending could be targeted on the poor and near-poor, including the disabled, pregnant women, and young children. This approach might reduce the cost of employer-paid insurance to some firms by covering many of the working poor under a public program. Work incentives would improve because Medicaid-covered individuals would not lose health benefits by taking a job, as they do under the current system.

Finally, the administrative structure for establishing Medicaid eligibility, defining benefits, and reimbursing providers is already in place. And state Medicaid programs have had reasonable success in controlling costs.

There are also disadvantages, however. First, the costs of a Medicaid expansion are likely to be very high for some states, particularly those that historically have not had broad eligibility and benefit coverage—typically the poorer states. Medicaid is already one of the largest and fastest growing items in state budgets. A second problem is that a Medicaid expansion under current arrangements would perpetuate and extend the current two-tier system in which the Medicaid-covered poor have more limited access than the middle class. Medicaid programs have historically been extremely aggressive in controlling costs by limiting coverage and payment rates. If, to keep taxes low, states continue to aggressively control spending, the result in many states will be even more limited access to providers.

The cost problem would be even greater if states were required to reimburse hospitals and physicians at levels comparable to Medicare, a move that would be expensive but which would at the same time reduce access barriers now faced by Medicaid recipients. In addition to increasing the cost of current service levels, higher reimbursement levels would increase utilization as access increased. Such an expansion would be even more costly to the extent that the greater attractiveness of Medicaid would induce some individuals to drop their private health insurance. One way to minimize displacement of private insurance is to incorporate a sliding-scale premium schedule that rises steeply with income, but this would also discourage the increase in coverage that a Medicaid expansion is designed to achieve.

Any system of health care reform adopted in the United States is likely to maintain a two-tier system, whether the reform approach is targeted or universal, because of the unwillingness of Americans to go to a single centralized system. The problem with a Medicaid bottom tier is that it is small, is perceived to cover welfare-dependent members of society, and lacks political power. This leads to pressures to underfund it, thus aggravating access problems. The challenge is to achieve a two-tier system in which the tier that includes the poor is large enough and politically strong enough to receive reasonable coverage.

A third disadvantage to further Medicaid expansion is that states are not likely by themselves to have much success in controlling growth in costs (in contrast to *payments*) because they do not control much of the health care market. Unless system costs were controlled through Medicare as well as private sector managed care initiatives, Medicaid programs would be forced to either keep up with rapidly expanding health care costs or continue to underpay in relative terms, with the resulting adverse effects on access.

Last, further Medicaid expansion would still leave many individuals without coverage. In addition to the near-poor who would be eligible under a sliding-scale approach but would still find the premiums too high to pay, over 11 million Americans with current incomes above 200 percent of poverty do not have health insurance (Holahan and Zedlewski 1991). Under most feasible sliding-scale premium arrangements, these individuals would not be eligible unless they paid the full premium. Although buying into a public program might be less expensive than purchasing a private policy, many people would still choose not to obtain coverage as long as the system was voluntary.

FEDERALIZING MEDICAID

A second way to achieve a targeted expansion in coverage would be to replace Medicaid with a federal program that covered low-income Americans, by financing full coverage of all Americans below the poverty line and permitting others to buy in on a sliding-scale basis.[1] Many different income thresholds and premium schedules are possible. Most of the advantages and disadvantages of further expanding Medicaid would also apply to this approach. However, federalization would eliminate the problem of states competing to keep benefits meager in order to keep taxes low. Financial and administrative burdens on states would also be reduced, and coordination between Medicare and Medicaid policies would be facilitated. Disadvantages in comparison to Medicaid expansion are that the administrative burden on the federal government would increase greatly and the advantage of "states as national laboratories" would disappear. Federal costs would rise substantially with a large portion of that increase, resulting in a mere shifting of the burden from states to the federal government.

EXPANDING MEDICARE

Another type of targeted expansion of health coverage would extend Medicare—the non-means-tested program for the elderly and the disabled on Social Security—to children and/or all disabled persons.

As a substitute for or in addition to changes in Medicaid, Medicare-based coverage of children would have several advantages.[2] First, a substantial portion of American children currently lack insurance coverage. A recent study found that only 57 percent of all children under the age of 18 were covered by private insurance for the full 28-month period of study (Nelson and Short 1990). If eligibility determination were based simply on age, Medicare expansion would be an administratively simple way to cover all children, because it is already a large, well-functioning program.

A universal public program for children would also take the burden off employers who now provide family coverage, making coverage for workers more affordable. Thus, a program aimed at children would make it easier to cover the remainder of the uninsured population, whether through employer mandates or through other programs to encourage employer participation.

Children are a relatively low-cost group to cover, and improving the health of young children is likely to reap considerable dividends to society in future years. Benefits such as inoculations and other preventive services, tailored to the needs of children could be added to Medicare. In addition, clinics and special in-school programs could be designed to improve access to services for children.

An expansion to all disabled persons would also address a serious structural problem in private insurance markets. While Medicare covers permanently and totally disabled persons who have received Social Security benefits for two years, the working disabled and those not yet eligible for Medicare often find it difficult to obtain coverage. Broader coverage of the disabled would take most high-risk individuals out of the private insurance market, reducing the affordability problem for employers. It may, however, be difficult to objectively define the group to be covered—e.g., would partially disabled individuals be covered?

An expanded Medicare program could be financed entirely through taxes or through taxes and modest premiums imposed on those covered. The current Medicare program imposes modest premiums on all who seek Part B coverage to cover some of the program cost. Similar, subsidized premiums could be imposed on children and the disabled, with premiums for the poor paid by the Medicaid program.

Expanding Medicare to cover children and/or all the disabled also has disadvantages. While this targeted expansion would help many of the uninsured who are often viewed as particularly "deserving," it would also displace private coverage that many children and disabled now have. The public sector costs and taxpayer burden would therefore be high relative to the increases in coverage that would be achieved. At the same time, substantial gaps in coverage would still remain. Low-income adults would remain particularly at risk, as would those who have "existing" acute care problems that make them identifiably bad risks.

Another disadvantage to this approach is that like Medicaid expansion, cost containment efforts likely would be confined to those to whom coverage has been expanded. These groups could be treated for purposes of cost containment just like other Medicare beneficiaries. But unless the expansion of coverage were large enough to make Medicare the largest payer for most of their services, the many activities for which Medicare does not have much market power would continue to fall outside the reach of any attempts to improve efficiency. Although special efforts could be made to improve cost containment strategies in conjunction with a Medicare expansion, the major thrust of such a proposal is to improve access rather than control costs.

EMPLOYER MANDATES

Most mandated approaches contain at least two basic elements: a required role for some or all employers to subsidize insurance for their employees, and an expansion of public-sector coverage to fill in the remaining gaps in coverage.[3] Variations on this basic proposal generally revolve around requirements to cover employees' families or exceptions aimed at protecting employers with a small number of employees or with part-time or low-wage workers.

Protections for certain employers often take the form of exemption from the mandate. Small businesses are often struggling to survive or are newly starting out and may find it difficult to obtain or afford health insurance. Thus, for example, employers with 20 or fewer employees might be relieved of the responsibility of offering coverage. Employer mandate proposals are also usually designed to protect employers with part-time and low-wage workers from inordinately high insurance costs. Employees who work only a few hours a week are exempted from the mandated insurance coverage, as are low-wage workers. The costs of insurance for employers of these workers may be a high enough proportion of the latter's wages that mandating coverage could have an important adverse impact on their chances of continued employment.

The major advantages of health care proposals that retain or enlarge the role of employers in providing health insurance coverage are practicality and retention of the status quo. Proponents of this type of approach usually do not embrace it as theoretically superior to others. Rather, they support it because it reflects the historical role of the private sector in health coverage and because it would minimize the direct financing of health care through the public sector.

The "Pay or Play" Approach

Excluding any categories of employers or workers, of course, defeats the purpose of providing universal coverage of the workforce. For this reason, other approaches to solve the problems of insuring part-time or low-wage workers and reducing the burdens on small business have also been proposed. The most frequently espoused variant is to provide employers the option of paying a tax instead of offering insurance to their employees. This is often referred to as the "pay or play" approach. In this case, employers could choose to pay a tax to enroll their employees in the public plan—probably the same plan that covers low-income persons who are not in the labor force. If the tax is tied to the wage cost, employers with low-wage workers would find it to their advantage to pay the tax, whereas employers with higher wage workers may prefer to provide insurance directly. As far as small firms are concerned, in order to keep in business—the main reason for excluding them from the mandate in the first place—the tax would have to be less of a burden than the cost of insurance purchased in the private market. Thus, the public plan would need to be subsidized by general revenue funds to make up the difference.

Such an approach is still less expensive to the government (though not to society as a whole) than picking up the full costs of low-wage and part-time workers through a Medicaid expansion. Moreover, under this approach, employers with high-wage workers would find it to their advantage to "play," that is, to offer insurance. This would retain the current system and move fewer people into a public plan than would other reform options aimed at universal coverage.

As noted above, the major advantage of this approach is the political one of minimizing the public sector role, since fewer new taxes would need to be raised. Insurance companies would also be somewhat mollified because much of their current role would be preserved. This approach would also help small businesses by reducing the administrative and cost burdens of offering insurance. Small businesses could simply pay the tax and avoid the paperwork—an advantage even if the tax would cost about the same as private insurance premiums.

Several groups have endorsed some form of the "pay or play" approach. The Pepper Commission recommendations, for example, would mandate all large employers (above 100 employees) to offer insurance or pay a tax (The Pepper Commission 1990). Small employers would be given tax incentives and insurance reforms aimed at improving their market. If small businesses do not voluntarily increase their provision of insurance, the "pay or play" mandate would eventually apply to them as well.

Ironically, however, the Pepper Commission's proposal would not offer small employers the option of buying into the public plan until their mandate is triggered. The public plan would cover all unemployed persons up to 100 percent of poverty and allow others up to 200 percent of poverty to buy in on a sliding scale. The public benefit package would be fairly limited (e.g., it would exclude prescription drugs), and would include a 20 percent co-insurance provision.

The National Leadership Commission has offered a similar plan (National Leadership Commission on Health Care 1989). In addition, the state of Massachusetts is attempting to implement its pay or play version though a statewide employer mandate (Intergovernmental Health Policy Project 1990). The plan is currently mired in political controversy, however, and Massachusett's currently poor economy is also a barrier to implementation.

A number of criticisms can be leveled at "pay or play" employer mandates. First, although mandates often give the impression that they will not interfere with the status quo for most families, the treatment of dependents in families with two workers in a mandated system could result in many changes in coverage. If all employers must offer insurance to their employees, how will overlapping coverage be handled? Families that now choose the better of the two insurance packages might find half their family members shifted to a different and perhaps inferior plan. In addition, under a "pay or play" system, a number of employers who now offer insurance might opt for the public plan, again causing major changes in the insurance coverage of the affected families. Except for the well-off with strong plans that may continue largely unchanged in a mandated system, few persons could count on no change.

<u>Second</u>, the indirect nature of a mandated system leaves open the question of whether there would be other types of reforms to help the efficiency of the current insurance market. Few observers of the health insurance situation in the United States would argue that the present system is working well. At a minimum, there is widespread recognition that reform of the small group market is becoming critical. Even insurance companies are beginning to call for regulatory controls to curb unreasonable selection and coverage practices. But a mandated system is inherently neutral in this regard. Thus, many mandated proposals call for regulatory reforms in tandem with the mandate, often in the form of community rating requirements—that all insured with a specified nonhealth-related set of characteristics be offered the same rate. This requirement would ensure that insurers offer coverage to employers with both healthy and high risk workers. Without such reform, insurers often compete selectively, and what appears to be price competition is only the exclusion of bad risks.

Without insurance reform, these undesirable behaviors on the part of insurers could also lead to a concentration of high-risk individuals in the public plan. If private insurers will not offer reasonable policies to some employers, their only choice might be the public "pay" option. If so, the tax on employers for the public plan might have to rise to cover what would become in effect a high-risk pool. Such a high tax would then give the erroneous impression that the public plan was inefficient compared to private insurance options.

Another downside of an employer mandated system is that it does not directly address the important issue of cost containment. Will a system of many competing insurance companies together with a modest public program result in effective controls on health care prices and volume growth? Growth in costs have already contributed to employers' reluctance to offer health insurance coverage. Unless the public sector portion were quite large, we would continue the very fragmented system we have today, which creates neither incentives for more efficient care nor regulations to help ensure that providers improve their efficiency. Mandating that they provide benefits without concern for cost containment may result in untenable burdens on employers over time.

The level of generosity of the basic employer-sponsored benefit package will also have major implications for health care costs. If the coverage requirements are minimal, many low-income citizens will still lack access to important services. On the other hand, the experience of many states that have already implemented employer mandates has been the reverse. In these states, various interest groups have managed to add their services to the list of required benefits, thus expanding mandated benefits. Under a mandated system much of the cost of new benefits is not felt directly by the government, making it tempting over time for policymakers to enrich the package. While mandated benefits would apply to the public program as well, unless that program were unexpectedly large in relation to the employer-based system, legislators would be more inclined toward the political advantages of largely costless generosity than toward concern for tax increases necessary to cover the increase in benefits in the public program.

As a consequence, mandated approaches, even when combined with expanded public sector coverage, are often viewed as insufficient. Below we turn to different approaches that would provide more comprehensive coverage for Americans.

MANDATES PLUS MANAGED CARE

In the economist's paradigm of a competitive market, there are many producers and many well-informed consumers. The knowledge and dollar power of the consumers and their ability to choose among producers forces producers to maximize efficiency and minimize cost in order to remain in business. Competition that promotes efficiency is clearly in the interest of society as a whole. But to the extent that insurers compete through favorable selection and cost shifting, the competition of private insurance companies impedes health care system efficiency.

The intent of approaches that include employer mandates plus managed care is to transform the health care market into one in which consumers have the well-informed buying power necessary to induce producer efficiency. It is important to note that in the health care context, the creation of a competitive market in this sense is not a *laissez faire* approach. Rather, it assumes that all the actors—employers, insurers, providers, and consumers—may need to face new rules before competition can be expected to work. This, in turn, assumes the intervention of government to help control the market through positive and negative incentives. Ironically, many of the advocates of using the market to discipline the health care system have moved over time from advocating less to advocating more government control in pursuit of their objectives.

To illustrate how this could work, we discuss a plan proposed by Alain Enthoven and Richard Kronick (1989). Their plan would provide universal coverage while maintaining employment-based insurance, Medicare, and Medicaid. The objective of universal coverage is to be achieved by "making the system affordable for all," certainly by providing financial protection for all and, if need be, by the creation of public providers as well. Though public sector costs would rise initially, the overall savings necessary to make this approach workable would ultimately come from the growth in efficient financing and delivery arrangements, which the authors assume will be demanded by consumers once they are given the necessary incentives to be cost-conscious.

Under this system, the mechanism through which increased consumer cost-consciousness and the buying power of the "public sponsor" (explained below) ultimately lowers costs is called *managed competition*. The essence of this idea is that large employers and public sponsors would coordinate the decisions of better-informed consumers regarding the choice of plans, in the expectation that health plans offering high-quality care at low costs would see enrollment increase and that health plans offering inferior and/or higher priced care would lose enrollment. To safeguard against the problem of adverse selection in managed competition, under the Enthoven-Kronick plan premiums would be "risk-rated" based on the expected costs of groups of individuals with similar characteristics. Health plans would receive larger payments when they enrolled individuals in higher risk groups.

Employers would be required by law to provide insurance to all full-time employees and to pay a tax on the wages and salaries of all other workers (i.e., part-time or seasonal workers). Employers would no longer be able to make unlimited tax-free payments for health insurance on behalf of their employees. Instead, employers would be required to make a defined payment independent of the health plan chosen, a payment that could only vary according to the health risk of the particular plan enrollees. This would make consumers more cost-conscious because employees who wanted to retain their more expensive insurance plan would have to pay the difference between their employer's old contribution and the more limited contribution with net after-tax dollars mandated under this system.

The major structural change Enthoven and Kronick propose is that each state be given strong incentives by the federal government to create agencies—called "public sponsors"—through which people otherwise uninsured could purchase coverage. These individuals would include self-employed workers and those not covered under the employer mandate. The public sponsors can be thought of as insurance brokers with the power to decide which plans are offered, to enter into contracts with the included plans, to administer enrollment, collect and disburse premiums, and to establish cross-subsidies among enrollees and the population as a whole. The public sponsors, thus, would have the ability to pool risks and achieve economies of scale. They would be administered by the states under federal guidelines, with costs shared by the federal government. In addition, the poor might be given income-based subsidies and small employers payroll-based subsidies to help cover the cost of publicly sponsored coverage.

The potential advantages of an Enthoven-Kronick type of proposal are clear. It would preserve the employment-based component of our system, provide every American with the financing necessary to buy health insurance coverage, and build real cost-control incentives into the system.

The disadvantages all have to do with whether the system would work as its designers intend. First, the ability to afford the expanded coverage depends upon the choice of efficient plans by individuals enrolled in the mandated private sector system. Implicit in this assumption is the belief that, given full information about plan quality and costs, consumers will opt for the low-cost alternative once the in-kind tax subsidies (in the form of employers' tax-exempt premium contributions) are reduced. However, there is no evidence to suggest that consumers will pick the low-cost option. Many, in fact, might be willing to pay more to keep their current health insurance arrangements in place. If most people select their present high-cost plans because of perceived access and/or quality advantages, in spite of having to bear the costs directly, the lower cost plans would not flourish. Second, the plan assumes that actuarily fair risk-rated premiums can be established and implemented. This may be very difficult to achieve in practice, resulting in continued competition to enroll the healthy and avoid the sick.

Finally, the political feasibility of this type of proposal is unclear. This system makes major changes in the tax treatment of employers' health insurance contributions that would adversely affect middle- and high-income, well-insured individuals. Moreover, although it leaves decisions to the private sector, it requires a substantial commitment of government resources to achieve its cost containment goals, which are the heart of the plan.

MANDATES AND A SINGLE RATE-SETTER OPTION

Instead of relying on incentives and market competition to control costs, another type of reform proposal would have the federal government or state directly control provider payments. These controls could limit both the prices paid for services *and* the volume of those services. The government would set payment rates that all payers would have to abide by. Many health analysts have envisioned such an approach as part of a universal public system. Such controls on provider payments could also be implemented in conjunction with a mixed public/private arrangement for offering coverage. Under this scenario, hospitals and physicians would have the same arrangements with an insurer such as Blue Cross/Blue Shield as with commercial insurers or Medicare. The payments, though not necessarily equal for all payers, would be set by the same authority, regardless of who provided the coverage.

Several states working with or in addition to Medicare (e.g., New York, New Jersey, Maryland, and Massachusetts) now operate systems that control payments for hospital services. The state sets rates for payments made directly by the insurer to the hospital. Payment is based on a per diem or a per diagnosis-related-group (DRG) basis, and source of coverage does not enter into the calculations. By explicitly not reimbursing on the basis of actual costs, hospitals are encouraged to be more efficient. Research shows that all-payer systems have successfully held down costs in these states (Zuckerman 1987).

Similar approaches could be taken to establish fees for physicians, perhaps by adopting the new fee schedules under development for Medicare. This would have physicians face the same fees for all patients and would reduce incentives to exclude some patients whose coverage is less generous.

But hospital rate setting and physician fee schedules may not necessarily go far enough in controlling costs. A single rate-setter system could also try to establish control over service volume. One way to do so would be to introduce broader-based payments—overall budgets for hospitals and capitated payments per patient to physicians, for example. These more dramatic payment schemes might avoid micro-management while adding volume controls to the system. Less dramatic arrangements can build in volume controls to the fee schedules, as Medicare is now attempting. These controls seek to limit growth in payments per service in response to inordinate growth in the number of services.

New York currently is considering an expanded rate-setting system. The Universal New York Care proposal would seek universal coverage through a "pay or play" system and an expanded public program for low-income persons (Beauchamp and Rouse 1990). Unlike state systems that control only hospital rates, a single-payer authority would handle all bills, paying providers and charging final payers. Thus, all revenues would flow through fiscal intermediaries hired to process claims. Insurance companies would collect the premiums from the insured. Uniform rates of reimbursement would be used and the system would move over time from fee-for-service to capitation-like budgeting, like the system already used by HMOs, which charge per person enrolled, not per service or per diagnosis. Case management is also suggested as a means to control costs.

The advantages of such a system are several. First, it would eliminate the current practice of some payers subsidizing others. Second, government would be able to bargain directly with hospitals and physicians—an approach that has already proven successful in controlling hospital costs. Third, it would give the public sector control over the diffusion of high-cost technology and over growth in service volume. Finally, the administrative simplification of dealing with a single rate-setter could help offset some resistance among health care providers. Current cost containment efforts by many different payers are likely to result in increasingly complex rules over time.

The major difficulty with this approach is that there is no agreement in the U.S. that a regulatory approach is best. Many believe that a decentralized approach, relying at least in part on market competition, would permit more flexibility in insurance arrangements while also controlling costs. In addition, critics of regulation often cite potential problems related to diminished quality of care. Without more agreement, it may not be politically feasible to move to a full regulatory approach.

Other disadvantages have to do with feasibility. The U.S. lacks physician, hospital, and other provider groups that could negotiate on behalf of all members of their group, particularly at the national level. Some European countries have such systems as part of their national health insurance, creating a direct avenue for negotiation that might make regulation more acceptable to providers.

MANDATES, SINGLE RATE-SETTER, AND A LARGE PUBLIC PROGRAM

The single rate-setter system described above offers direct government control over the provider side of health care. Under this system, insurance companies, HMOs, PPOs, and IPAs serve mainly as conduits for the financing of employer-based coverage. If the basic package offered to individuals is fixed, there is little to be gained from retaining private insurance. If the basic package is not largely fixed, some of the control over costs may be lost as insurance companies compete to offer packages that may encourage adverse selection or other less productive competition.

To minimize unproductive competition it may be desirable to combine such a system with a large public insurance pool. Under this option, an explicit goal could be to exclude very high-income persons from public sector insurance. These persons are likely to have generous benefits under our current system and a lot to lose under a public system. One of the criticisms of expanding health insurance coverage through a large public program is that those who now have very good coverage would either be strong opponents of this change or would force the public program to be extremely generous, and thus extremely expensive. If there are provisions for higher income persons to opt out of the system, some of the pressures for "Cadillac care" would be eased. At the same time, the public tier would still be large enough to be viewed as a mainstream health program rather than simply a welfare benefit for the poor.

This type of two-tier system could be achieved with a "pay or play" system in which the employer payroll-based tax rate was set low enough for many employers to find it less expensive to pay than to play. Employers choosing to purchase private insurance would be the ones who wanted to offer very generous coverage or had very high-wage employees.

Of course, in order to keep the employer tax low enough to raise participation in the public plan, other taxes would be needed to subsidize the plan. But spreading the burden of helping lower income workers with their health insurance coverage beyond employers to taxpayers in general would reduce the negative employment impacts on low-wage workers, because employers would not bear the full cost of the plan.

With this large public plan, the government could presumably combine some of its access and cost containment goals into one efficient system, eliminating some of the marketing and administrative costs of the private sector. And it would do so without forcing *everyone* into one public plan. The safety valve allowed by the second tier of private benefits could help hold down demand for "Cadillac care" and could allow for experimentation in new coverage and types of care arrangements. But the basic idea is that even those in the second, private tier would be governed by the single rate-setting agent.

One obvious disadvantage of this approach is that the larger the pool in the public plan, the larger the subsidy needed and the larger the required increase in general taxes. In addition, this approach may call for a more regulatory approach than would be politically feasible.

UNIVERSAL PUBLIC APPROACHES

In some ways, the simplest type of reform would be to move to a universal public system. Everyone would receive their coverage through the government and all providers would negotiate with the government for compensation. This approach would not try to salvage what many view as an ailing private sector approach, but would make more sweeping changes. The reason we place it at the complex end of our list of reform proposals is because it would constitute a monumental change from the current system.

An example of a universal public system would be the expansion of Medicare to the entire nonelderly population. This could be achieved through the current Medicare structure that consists of a federally administered program funded with a combination of premiums and federal taxes. Alternatively, a universal public system could be modeled after the Canadian system, with joint federal/state administration and financing.

The advantages are several. By definition, a universal public system would solve the problem of the uninsured. All Americans would be in the same system. There would be no shifting between plans with changes in employment and no gaps in coverage. (If premium contributions were

required, some persons might choose to remain uninsured. The program might then have to mandate insurance coverage to assure everyone is covered under the
system.) The decision about who would pay would be
made explicitly, through the tax system, rather than im-
plicitly as the burden is now distributed.

The major problem with a universal public program,
as noted earlier, is the extremely large tax burden that it
would necessitate. Reasonable estimates suggest that the
increased tax burden would amount to $220 to $250
billion. These revenues would not all represent new costs
to society as a whole. The funds would largely replace
employer premiums, employee contributions, private payments for insurance policies, and direct out-of-pocket
costs for health care. The distribution of burdens across
individuals would depend on the kind of tax structure
established to pay for the program. Who would pay how
much for health insurance would clearly be very different
than it is now.

In the aggregate, the total financial burden on Americans could be lower under a universal public system. The
administrative costs of a public system would be lower
than under a mixed public/private system. The administrative costs to hospitals, physicians, and other providers
would be reduced because of a uniform set of paperwork
requirements. It is estimated that if the U.S. had the
administrative cost burden of the Canadian system, U.S.
costs would drop from $80 billion to $50 billion, or by
about .5 percent of GNP (Himmelstein and Woolhandler
1986). Furthermore, providers would be faced with a
uniform set of benefits and coverage guidelines rather
than a multitude of differing utilization review criteria
imposed by many different insurers. Hospitals and phy-

sicians might prefer the administrative simplicity of one payment system and one set of utilization standards to the multitude of payment rates and utilization criteria inherent in the multiple-payer system we now have.

⌐In addition, the ability to control costs might be significantly enhanced. Medicare has established payment systems that could be expanded to the entire population. The Prospective Payment System (PPS) is well established for hospitals and could be adopted more broadly. Medicare is also moving to develop a payment system for outpatient care, and Congress has recently adopted a relative value scale for physician payment and is developing a system of volume performance standards that offers promise for controlling the volume of physician services. Professional review organizations are already established to monitor hospital admissions and lengths of stay. A universal public system could use these and other existing technical tools, together with the monopsony power of a large buyer, to control costs of hospital and physician services.⌐

A universal public system would also have some major advantages to employers. Firms would be free of the burden of providing health benefits and thereby relieved of the large administrative task of providing choices of plans, dealing with employee complaints, administering periods of open enrollment, and so on. The universal public system would also have advantages for the functioning of U.S. labor markets. Health insurance would not be a direct cost to employers. Employee decisions on job choice would be made independent of decisions concerning the availability of health insurance.

A uniform system does raise the thorny issue of whether all Americans should be under the same system. It would be difficult to design a set of benefits that would be satisfactory to everyone. A minimum benefit package would be unsatisfactory to those who currently have broad coverage, while a rich benefit package would be too expensive. Therefore, the question is whether a one-tier system is feasible or desirable. As noted, the policy could allow for a small upper tier for individuals who wished to use their own resources to pay for private insurance.

In Canada, private insurance is not allowed for services covered by the public plan (Iglehart 1990). But it is difficult to believe that private insurance could be made illegal in this country. Indeed, the downsizing of the private insurance system would almost certainly prove to be a major political obstacle to the enactment of a universal public system. However, the risk of retaining even a downsized private system is that the remaining private insurance sector could cream off the good risks, leaving the public system to insure the lower income and higher risk individuals. This might be avoided if all Americans, whether purchasing private insurance or not, were required to pay payroll, income, or consumption taxes to finance the public insurance system. Such a system would be analogous to the financing of public schools in the United States: these taxes would be sufficiently large so that relatively few could afford private coverage, just as relatively few can afford private schools. (It would of course differ in that medical care would still be largely provided by the private, not the public sector, as with education.)

Another way to incorporate multiple tiers within the system is to permit hospitals or physicians to choose participation status. Participating physicians would be paid in full at the system's fees or rates; nonparticipants would be paid some percentage of the fee schedule or hospital rate. Individuals who choose to go to nonparticipants would be expected to pay more for the luxury of broader choice.

One major issue with respect to a universal system is whether it should be administered by the federal government or jointly by the federal and state governments. A purely federal program would require uniformity across states, and would entail a very large administrative and financial role for the federal government. While this would relieve states of a major administrative and financial burden, such uniformity across states may not be realistic in this country. What is more likely to work here is a joint federal/state system that would allow for differences across states that reflect political differences in viewpoints regarding market competition and regulation.

The disadvantage to a joint federal/state program is that it would be dependent upon state administrative capacity, which currently varies from outstanding to relatively weak. Also, since a joint system might come to reflect differences in coverage and benefits emanating from differences in incomes and attitudes toward redistribution of well-being, a joint federal/state program would require some difficult decisions about what must be uniform. For example, in Canada, the provinces may not impose cost sharing and must accept limits on balance billing (Iglehart 1990).

As noted earlier, a universal public system could be unacceptable to Americans used to private markets and a wide range of choice. Such a system might not be able to respond to differences in need and preferences across geographic areas, and might fail to properly reward differences in quality among hospitals and abilities among physicians. A system heavily reliant on tax financing could be under- or over-financed. On the one hand, the system could be so successful in controlling costs that quality of care problems would arise. Ideally, such problems would lead the citizenry to be willing to increase tax contributions to the system, but there is no assurance that this would occur. On the other hand, special interests, hospitals, and physician organizations—being better organized than consumer/taxpayers—might succeed in obtaining increases in payment rates, leading to failure of the system's ability to control spending.

Notes, chapter 3

1. The Reagan administration included such a proposal in its federalism initiative. More recently, this option has been discussed as part of other proposals, such as that of the Pepper Commission.

2. Congressman Pete Stark (D., Ca.) has proposed legislation that would expand Medicare-style, non-means-tested coverage to pregnant women and children.

3. A number of proposals would include employer mandates in some form. One of the best known has been proposed by Senator Edward Kennedy (D., Ma.) and Congressman Henry Waxman (D., Ca.). Different versions of these proposals have been introduced in Congress.

4

AN AMERICAN APPROACH TO REFORM

A ny serious proposal for health system reform must provide insurance coverage for all Americans. It must also establish credible incentives and mechanisms for cost control in a way that recognizes the diversity of opinion on what strategies work best. And it must be structurally and politically realistic within the American context. The following approach, in our judgment, meets all of these criteria.

MEDICARE REMAINS UNCHANGED

The first component of the proposal is that Medicare would be unchanged. Medicare is the major health insurance program for aged and disabled Social Security recipients; it is administered federally and has uniform national policies. The program is well-established and highly popular. There is little to be gained from altering its structure. However, it will be necessary to continue the process of developing cost-containment strategies that Medicare has already begun, because the program faces major financial problems over the coming years.

EMPLOYERS "PAY OR PLAY"

The second component is a "pay or play" scheme—requiring employers to either provide private health insurance to their workers or to pay a tax that will be used to create back-up public health insurance programs to cover workers (and the poor) not covered by private plans. Insurers would be required to offer policies at community rates that could vary for broad groups of individuals; they would also be prohibited from pre-existing condition exclusions and other means of avoiding high risk enrollees. All firms except those with fewer than a specified number of employees would be required to provide health insurance to all employees working more than a certain number of hours per week. The objective would be to cover all firms where administratively practical. One approach would be to include all employers now paying the F.I.C.A. tax; this would then include employers with even one employee. Part-time workers could also be covered through the employer payroll tax, ensuring nearly universal coverage.

Employers would be required to provide health insurance meeting minimum standards in terms of benefits, with legislatively established deductibles and coinsurance; employers would be required to pay at least 75 percent of the cost of this coverage.[1] Employers could offer more generous plans but the difference in actuarial value between the offered plan and the required benefits would be treated as taxable employee income. Employees would be required to purchase insurance for themselves and their families if offered by the employer; individuals with incomes below certain specified levels would have the costs of private insurance subsidized by the state.

Most basic acute care services including cost effective preventive services would be covered; prescription drugs would be excluded, at least initially. Annual deductibles would be approximately $200 per person and $500 per family, with coinsurance equal to 20 percent up to annual catastrophic limits of approximately $1500 per individual and $3000 per family. Individuals and families below certain income levels could be exempt from cost sharing or have lower catastrophic limits.

STATE PUBLIC PROGRAMS REPLACE MEDICAID

Firms not wishing to provide such private policies would be required to pay a tax approximately equal to the national average percentage of payroll now devoted to health insurance, about 7.0 percent. Firms could choose to offer a private plan for full-time workers and to pay the tax for part-time workers but otherwise must choose one approach for all employees. States would be required to use these payroll tax revenues to establish new back-up public health insurance programs. These new programs would provide insurance for workers whose employers choose to pay the tax and would also replace Medicaid for persons not in the workforce. The new public programs would provide coverage to all nonworking individuals and their families with incomes below poverty at no cost to the individual or the families. Individuals and families with incomes between 100 and 250 percent of the poverty line would be permitted to purchase this insurance on a sliding scale. Those with higher incomes could buy into the public plan at the full community-rated cost. Once affordable coverage is offered to all individuals, enrollment could be required so that everyone contributes to the cost of their health care.

The tax would be set at a rate that would result in a large minority of employers choosing to pay it rather than provide private insurance. (The exact rate that would yield the desired mix of private- and public-plan enrollees would depend on the cost of the mandated plan and the distribution of payroll expenses across firms.) A relatively large public program, containing about one-third of the non-elderly, would ensure the establishment of provider payment standards that are high enough to create acceptable levels of access to voters, many of whom would also be program participants. We would prefer to rely on the political power that a sizable number of public-plan enrollees would provide to ensure that adequate minimum standards of quality and access are established. The alternative would be detailed federal rules and regulations for state-administered programs. If reliance on the political process results in inadequate access for public-plan enrollees, some minimum standards for provider reimbursement and utilization control may be necessary. Our concern, however, is that overly rigid requirements will limit state flexibility in the design of cost containment strategies.

Firms with relatively healthy, highly paid employees would probably choose to offer a private plan. Firms with large numbers of low-wage or part-time employees, or with disproportionate numbers of older workers or individuals in poor health, as well as firms wishing to avoid the administrative burden of purchasing health insurance, would probably choose to pay the tax. Because health care costs and, thus, private insurance premiums will be high (or low) in the same markets where payrolls tend to be high (or low), there should not be major geographic differences in incentives to choose the public plan.

The public programs that replace Medicaid would therefore cover three types of persons: 1) workers whose employers pay the tax, 2) the poor, and 3) families and individuals who buy into the public plan. The program would be financed by the tax on employers, by limitations on the tax-free status employer health insurance contributions, by sliding scale beneficiary contributions, and by federal and state subsidies.

An essential feature of our approach to controlling cost growth is that the percentage increase in the federal contribution each year will be equal to the growth in nominal gross national product, as is done in Canada.[2] The federal contribution would initially vary from 50 to 75 percent of the cost of subsidizing the public program, with the federal contribution varying inversely with state per capita income, and varying directly with the number of persons in poverty. On average, the federal government contribution would be about 60 percent of the total cost. The federal contribution could be financed by an earmarked tax such as a national sales tax or a payroll tax. While it is not essential that the federal contribution be earmarked, the federal contribution rate does need to increase in step with inflation and long-term real growth in the economy. It is also important that a mechanism be established to protect states from short-term declines in income during periods of economic downturn.

COST

Because this proposal has some important features in common with the Pepper Commission plan, the cost estimates for the latter ($24 billion) offer some guidance as to the cost of our approach. Our proposal would cover approximately 35 percent of the nonelderly population in the public plan, necessitating higher federal and state taxes (relative to the Pepper plan) beyond the payroll taxes. Both the cost of subsidizing non-workers and dependents below 250 percent of the poverty line (including the cost of increasing reimbursement rates for current Medicaid beneficiaries), and the cost of subsidizing those whose employers choose to pay the tax would be somewhat higher than in the Pepper Commission proposal. Offsetting these costs, however, would be the increase in federal (and possibly state) tax revenues from the limitations on the tax-free status of employer health insurance premiums (lowering tax expenditures). Estimation of these costs, as well as costs of all "pay or play" proposals, including that of the Pepper Commission, is complicated because of the lack of good data on the distribution of payroll expenses across firms. With regard to these cost estimates, however, two issues merit serious attention. First, much of our increased public costs would be offset by reductions in the costs of privately purchased health insurance, out-of-pocket expenses, and uncompensated care. Second, the more important cost issue is the growth in health expenditures over time. The savings gained from getting expenditure growth under control could well compensate for the additional first-year reform costs. ⌐

THE BURDEN ON STATES

The effect of the cost containment provisions is that if increases in medical care costs exceed the rate of growth in GNP, states would, by design, bear an increasingly large burden for the cost of health care. The objective, in addition to sharing the burden of financing the system between both the federal and state governments, is to provide strong incentives for states to control costs by having them bear a measure of financial risk for failure. States could, of course, lobby to have the federal contribution tax rate increased.

States would have the freedom to choose among a variety of strategies for cost containment. We believe this freedom is essential because there are fundamental disagreements on how the system's costs should be contained. For example, states could choose an Enthoven-Kronick type of approach to managed competition, allowing private insurance entities such as PPOs and HMOs to compete to control costs. This could include permitting the public programs to buy individuals into private insurance arrangements. Alternatively, states could choose to use some form of all-payer rate setting, such as the Universal New York Health Care (UNY*CARE) approach, to control both price and volume of care. These regulations would be applied to both public and private sector plans. They could also choose to limit coverage to cost effective procedures along the lines that have recently been proposed in Oregon. States would also have Medicare policies available as a possible model.

States' incentives for cost containment would extend beyond the risk of excess growth in the costs of the care of public-plan enrollees. States would also have incentives to be concerned with the growth in costs of private plans. If private insurance premiums increase as a percentage of payroll, employers will be more inclined to pay the tax than to offer private insurance. This will increase the number of enrollees in the public plan, thereby increasing the need for state (and federal) subsidies. This should also serve as an incentive to the private insurance industry to control the growth in health care costs and thus premiums, because failure to do so will mean loss of market share and an increase in public plan enrollment. Finally, because insurance reforms would limit risk-selection opportunities, cost control must come through controlling provider payments and increased administrative efficiency.

Lightening the Burden

The increase in costs for states would represent a relatively large financial burden for many of them. One way to alleviate this burden would be to federalize the long-term care component of the Medicaid program. This would provide approximately $14.5 billion of fiscal relief to states, in 1990 dollars. (While this is approximately the same amount as the increase in states' costs for the expansion of acute care, there would be gainers and losers among individual states, an issue that may need to be addressed.) Long-term care is a large burden for states, and one that will grow substantially over time as the population ages. Relieving states of this burden may make the added responsibilities for administering the acute care system more acceptable. Federalizing long-term care would also facilitate the coordination of Medicare and Medicaid policies on nursing homes and home health care.

CONCLUSION

In sum, in terms of the six questions laid out in chapter 2, this plan addresses the following dimensions:

1. It would *cover everyone*. The elderly would be covered by Medicare; some workers and dependents by employer-based coverage, and the poor, unemployed, and other workers and dependents through a state-level public program that would replace Medicaid.

2. It would *control costs* through legislative requirements regarding deductibles and coinsurance, and by giving the states a substantial financial stake in ensuring that public program costs do not grow faster than general inflation. State control would also allow the testing of different mechanisms for cost control, with the ultimate objective of identifying the most effective cost containment strategies.

3. *The cost would be borne by employers, employees, and taxpayers.* Employers would be protected from exorbitant costs by being allowed the option of paying into

a public plan rather than providing private health insurance themselves. The poor and unemployed would be protected by having their public program coverage subsidized on a sliding scale.

4. *There would be a standard minimum package of required benefits* for employer-based and public programs, with legislative requirements on maximum cost sharing. Choice of provider might be restricted in some states.

5. *Administration* of the private programs would be the responsibility, as now, of employers and/or insurance companies. Administration of the public program would be the responsibility of the states, with the objective of maximizing responsiveness to local needs and conditions.

6. *The political feasibility test would be met* by retaining a major role for insurance companies and by retaining the role of employer-based coverage, thus reducing the tax increase needed to ensure universal coverage. By allowing flexibility in design of cost containment strategy, some of the current controversy over this issue would also be deflected.

Our proposal is not without its problems. First, our approach would still have adverse effects on the profitability of small businesses and on the employment prospects for low-wage workers, although these effects would be less than under conventional mandates and less than under proposals with higher tax rates. Second, some states may not want the responsibility we envision, or have the capacity to carry it out. But several Canadian provinces are relatively small and are able to perform the same administrative functions within the Canadian national health system. In addition, since the federal government would continue to administer the Medicare program, states would have the option of tying their policies on public program hospital and physician payment and utilization control to those of Medicare.

Finally, the proposal would mean a significant increase in taxes. Some of this would replace funds spent at the local level to finance public hospital deficits and to reduce uncompensated care in other hospitals. Some of it would also replace expenditures borne by corporations in purchasing private health insurance plans, and some would replace the insurance premiums privately borne by individuals. Nonetheless, the plan would entail a visible increase in taxes at the federal and state levels. In our view, this increase seems a modest price to pay for resolving the problem of the uninsured and for gaining control over escalating costs now endemic to the U.S. health care system.

Notes, chapter 4

1. Employee Retirement Income Security Act rules would have to be modified to ensure that these provisions and others apply to those firms who currently choose to underwrite their own health insurance costs.

2. Because the kinds of individuals (i.e., high or low health risk) who will shift into the public plan are not easily predictable, some delay in the implementation of the indexing features of this proposal may be necessary.

REFERENCES

"1990 Annual Report." Board of Trustees of Federal Hospital Insurance Trust Fund, Washington, D.C., April 18, 1990.

Beauchamp, Dan E., and Ronald L. Rouse. 1990. "Universal New York Health Care: A Single-Payer Strategy Linking Cost Control and Universal Access." *New England Journal of Medicine* 323 (September 6): 562-568.

Berenson, Robert, and John Holahan. 1990. "Using a New Type of Service Classification System to Examine the Growth in Medicare Physician Expenditures, 1985 to 1988." Urban Institute Working Paper 3983-03, December.

DiCarlo, Steven, and Jon Gabel. 1988. "Conventional Health Plans: A Decade Later." *Health Insurance Association of America Research Bulletin* (November).

DiCarlo, Steven, and Jon Gabel. 1989. "Conventional Health Insurance: A Decade Later." *Health Care Financing Review* 10, no. 3 (Spring): 77-89.

Eby, Charles, and Donald Cohodes. 1985. "What Do We Know About Rate-Setting?" *Journal of Health Politics, Policy, and Law* 10 (Summer): 289-327.

Enthoven, Alain, and Richard Kronick. 1989. "A Consumer Choice Health Plan for the 1990s." *New England Journal of Medicine* 320 (January 5, Part I, and January 12, Part II).

Evans, Robert G. 1986. "Finding the Levers, Finding the Courage: Lessons from Cost Containment in North America." *Journal of Health Politics, Policy and Law* 11 (Winter): 585-615.

Evans, Robert G. et al. 1989. "Controlling Health Expenditures: The Canadian Reality." *New England Journal of Medicine* 320, no. 9 (March 2): 571-599.

Farley, Pamela J. 1985. "Who Are the Uninsured?" *Milbank Memorial Fund Quarterly* 63 (Summer): 476-503.

Fuchs, Victor, and James Hahn. 1990. "How Does Canada Do It?" *New England Journal of Medicine* 323 (September 27): 884-890.

GAO. 1990. "Health Insurance: Cost Increases lead to Coverage Limitations and Cost Shifting." GAO/HRD 90-68 (May) Washington, D.C.: General Accounting Office.

Himmelstein, David V., and Steffie Woolhandler. 1986. "Cost Without Benefit: Administrative Waste in U.S. Health Care." *New England Journal of Medicine* 314 (February 13): 441-445.

Holahan, John, and Sheila Zedlewski. 1991. "Expanding Medicaid to Cover Uninsured Americans." *Health Affairs* 10, no. 1 (Spring).

Iglehart, John K. 1990. "Canada's Health Care System Faces Its Problems." *New England Journal of Medicine* 322 (February 22): 562-568.

Intergovernmental Health Policy Project, George Washington University. 1990. "Massachusetts Health Security Act is on Track and on Time, Dukakis Reports." *State Health Notes* (March).

Lohr, Kathleen et al. 1986. "Use of Medical Care in the RAND Health Insurance Experiment." *Medical Care* 24 (September): 574-577.

Monhiet, Alan, and Pamela Short. 1989. "Mandatory Health Coverage." *Health Affairs* 8, no. 1 (Winter).

Morell, Virginia. 1990. "Oregon Puts Bold Health Plan on Ice." *Science* 249 (August 3): 468-471.

Moyer, Eugene. 1989. "A Revised Look at the Number of Uninsured Americans." *Health Affairs* 8, no. 2 (Summer).

National Leadership Commission on Health Care. 1989. *For the Health of a Nation: A Shared Responsibility.* Ann Arbor: Health Administration Press.

Nelson, Charles, and Kathleen Short. 1990. "Health Insurance Coverage 1986-1988." Current Population Reports, Household Economic Studies, Series P-70, no. 17 (March). Washington, D.C.: Bureau of the Census, U.S. Department of Commerce.

Poulier, Jean-Pierre. 1989. "Health Care Expenditures and Other Data." *Health Care Financing Review* 11, no. 1 (Fall).

ProPAC. 1990. *Medicine Prospective Payment and the American Health Care System: Report to the Congress.* Washington, D.C.: Prospective Payment Assessment Commission. June.

Robert Wood Johnson Foundation. 1987. *Access to Health Care Special Report No. 2.* Princeton, N.J.: Robert Wood Johnson Foundation.

Schieber, George J., and Jean-Pierre Poulier. 1989. "Overview of International Comparisons of Health Care Expenditures." *Health Care Financing Review* 11, no. 1 (Fall).

Starr, Paul. 1982. *The Social Transformation of American Medicine.* New York: Basic Books.

Swartz, Katherine. 1989. *The Medically Uninsured: Special Focus on Workers.* Washington, D.C.: The Urban Institute, July.

The Pepper Commission (U.S. Bipartisan Commission on Comprehensive Health Care). 1990. *A Call for Action.* Final Report, Washington, D.C.: U.S. Government Printing Office (September).

U.S. Department of Labor, Bureau of Labor Statistics. 1990. News, USDL 90-160 (March 30).

Zedlewski, Sheila R. 1991. *Expanding the Employer-Provided Health Insurance System: Effects on Workers and Their Employers.* UI Report 91-3, Washington, D.C.: The Urban Institute Press.

Zuckerman, Stephen. 1987. "Rate-Setting and Hospital Cost-containment: All-Payer versus Partial-Payer Approaches." *Health Services Research* 2 (August): 307-326.